RUNAWAYS LONDON

FOR THE ENSLAVED FREEDOM-SEEKERS OF THE 17TH AND 18TH CENTURIES

Edited by
Fahad Al-Amoudi
&
Kate Birch

Published by Ink Sweat & Tears Press
in association with Spread the Word
and the University of Glasgow's
Runaway Slaves in Britain project.

London 2021

Editors: Fahad Al-Amoudi and Kate Birch
Typeset and design by Starfish Limited
Printed and bound Micropress Printers Limited

William Morris, *The Earthly Paradise*, F.S. Ellis (1868)

Fred Moten, *The Feel Trio*, Letter Machine Editions (2014)

Simon P. Newman, 'Runaway London: history, storytelling and escape from slavery in 17th and 18th century London', (unpublished essay 2020), pp. 50-51

Solmaz Sharif, excerpt from 'Look' from *Look: Poems*. Copyright © 2016 by Solmaz Sharif. Reprinted with the permission of The Permissions Company, LLC on behalf of Graywolf Press, graywolfpress.org

Derek Walcott, 'Dread Song', *The Poetry of Derek Walcott 1948 -2013*, Selected by Glyn Maxwell, Faber & Faber Ltd (2019)

Historical Images:

The London Gazette 1701 – 1726 (Inner Covers)

Joannes de Ram, Londini Angliæ regni metropolis novissima & accuratissima (Amsterdam, 1690). University of Michigan, Clark Library. Clark Library regards this image as being in public domain. (Inner Covers)

ISBN 978-0-9927253-6-5

To Deago, Sabinah, Mary, Jean, Goude, Othello, Cato, Robin and all the named and unnamed in the runaway slave advertisements of 17th and 18th century London and to all those who did not take that route but continued to show resistance in their own ways

Between the 1650s and 1780s many hundreds of enslaved people were brought to London. Most were African although a significant minority were South Asian and a smaller number were indigenous American. While in the capital, some attempted to escape and, on occasions, those who pursued them placed advertisements in London newspapers seeking the capture and return of these freedom-seekers. The average age of the runaways was 16.

These 'runaway advertisements' reveal the existence of enslaved people in London yet tell us very little about them, and all through the eyes of those who enslaved and pursued them. Taking the dedicated historical research of Professor Simon Newman and the work on the history and heritage of slavery by Dr. Peggy Brunache as the starting point, Runaways' lead artists – poets Momtaza Mehri and Gboyega Odubanjo and illustrator Olivia Twist – alongside emerging poets Abena Essah, Oluwaseun Olayiwola and Memoona Zahid and artist Tasia Graham – have reimagined the stories of London's runaways, showing them as actors of resistance and resilience. They will be able to claim and represent this history on their own terms.

The Runaways London Project includes a film of the commissioned work and the research, and a resource pack for young people.

The project is managed by Spread the Word and the project publisher is Ink Sweat & Tears Press. The University of Glasgow is the main project partner.

Runaways London is supported and funded by: The British Association for American Studies/United States Embassy Small Grants Programme; Economic and Social Research Council, Impact Acceleration Award; University of Glasgow Knowledge Exchange (KE) Small Grants 2020/21; City of London Grants and through private donations.

TABLE OF CONTENTS

INTRODUCTION

Tower Hill, London, mid-September 1655. A child, who had likely been born in Africa, melted into the darkness of the City of London. We do not know his name: all we know is that he was described as 'a Negro Boy' who was 'about 14 years of age', that he was wearing 'a blew livery' and a periwig, and that he was the enslaved property of Lord Willoughby of Parham. We know this because Willoughby placed an advertisement in a London newspaper offering a reward for this youth's capture and return. The sixty-four words of this newspaper advertisement constitute the only known historical record of this unnamed child's existence. A wealth of documentary evidence illuminates the life of Lord Willoughby, the man who claimed ownership of this youth. But the gaps in the archive effectively silence this unnamed child, and we know of him only through the words written by Willoughby

He was one of thousands of enslaved Africans, South Asians and indigenous Americans who were brought to London and the British Isles more generally between the mid-seventeenth and late-eighteenth centuries. Some, like this unnamed youth, took their lives into their own hands by attempting to escape, hoping to forge new lives in freedom. Simon Newman's *Runaway Slaves in Britain* project has collected and published online many hundreds of eighteenth-century newspaper advertisements for enslaved people who escaped.

Many of the enslaved had been brought to the city as the personal servants of merchants, aristocrats, ships' captains and the other Londoners who were engaged in the developing slave trade and in England's colonies and trading settlements in Africa, the Americas and Asia. Contemporary portraits of wealthy Londoners often show them with well-dressed young Black attendants, many of them little more than children. They were human accessories, intended to show the wealth and success of the people who owned them. This kind of slavery was very different from the slavery experienced on Middle Passage ships travelling to the Americas or on the plantations where the enslaved endured short and brutal lives. Those held in London were the property of people who could—and sometimes did—send them to the plantations. Under this persistent threat and fearful of the relentless violence of colonial slavery, some of London's enslaved attempted to escape.

What were the lives of enslaved people seeking freedom in London like? What did they hope for when they absconded? Traditional historical research and writing cannot easily answer these questions: we can speculate, but in the end we just don't know. Our not knowing, and our inability to know, is the *raison d'être* for this project and book. This collection of poetry and art creatively imagines the lives of all those enslaved within London in the 17th and 18th centuries, whose resistance is still palpable.

Working with Ruth Harrison and Tom MacAndrew from Spread the Word, and with Kate Birch, Fahad Al-Amoudi and Desree at Ink Sweat & Tears, we have developed the *Runaways* project. We had two linked objectives. First, we sought to work with young creative artists of African, Caribbean and South Asian heritage, sharing with them historical research about London's freedom-seekers and empowering them to develop work inspired by those histories. We wanted them to imagine what might fill some of the archival gaps and silences and bring these people to life. Second, we hoped that for these artists, and for others who engage with their work, this project will increase awareness and understanding of this chapter in the history of London. This book showcases the work of these remarkable poets and artists, with some of the research that has inspired them.

Simon P. Newman and Peggy Brunache

MOMTAZA MEHRI

A Negro Man named Deago, run away the 4th Instant from his Master Capt. Benjamin Stowe, Commander of the Ship Charles. Whoever secures the Negro, and gives notice to the said Captain, or to Mr. Crisp at the Carolina Coffee-house in Birchin-lane, London, shall have 5 Guineas, and Charges.

— The London Gazette, 14th April 1701

I began this project by revisiting my fascination with the writings and abolitionist contributions of Olaudah Equiano, Ignatius Sancho and Ottobah Cugoano. Of course, constraint and compromise defined the Black authorial voice of the time. The political motivations and financial whims of patrons, publishers and beneficiaries all shaped the careers and lives of these figures. To me, it became clear that Black life during the tumultuous seventeenth and eighteenth centuries could not be measured in exceptions. I was curious about the daily realities of London's Black population. My challenge was to intimate the unknown and unspoken. I wanted to elaborate on archival silences and learn more about the Black people who did not make the history books — those whose presence could be witnessed on city streets, dockyards, inns, markets, and public houses. I was interested in how they negotiated difference; their diverse origins, their freedom (or lack thereof), the varying paths that had led them to London, and their often hostile surroundings.

The runaway advertisements demanded close reading. Hundreds appeared across London newspapers, listing enslaved people as property. Those in bondage shared column space with missing livestock notices, peddled goods, and sale items. The dehumanisation behind these concise blocks of text is glaring, but so is the underlying context. Every advertisement is a testament to an audacious desire for freedom that could not be suppressed, even under limitless terror. Each escape reaffirmed a humanity that had been denied. Could these runaways speak for themselves, without patronage or pageantry? What worlds did they build with their fragile freedom? What had they given up to be free?

These poems are imaginative interventions. They conjure the inner lives and webs of affiliation that might have sustained these runaways. They are attempts to resurrect fragments of our collective history.

Bankside, Breaking

more sorrow, less shame
more talk of the River that wash out my name

— Derek Walcott, 'Dread Song'

River Lea issues forth. A swelling lament. I forgive myself for what others have done. Limehouse, your workers burn like your kilns. I hide my open face from both. Lungfuls of docklands smoke besiege the chest. Sulphur lines the throat's walls. From here, the water is a blanket of possibility. Risk is gloriously circumstantial. Shorn of livery & lace, I inhale the fugitive smog, few possessions to weigh down this inconspicuous uniform of tatters. Mine, all mine. The ever-mushrooming city opens its slack jaws. Swallows its driftless dreamers whole. I disappear into its mouth and call this a beginning. Harbinger of private catastrophes, I bow my cap to you. We stand alongside each other, this river and I. As ever. Shamefully aware of how little we know of each other. Gut pulls at memoried knot, at the thread of a yet forgotten crisp morning. The day I first spotted a cormorant's inky glide across the port, I looked up at the sky, at the boundless flock above, and knew what banishment meant. We are a remembering people.

We have no other choice.

Reclamations

No longer child
No longer Monday's firstborn
No longer carrying the day's exultations
No longer embraced by broad-leaved belt of forest
No longer at the lush edge of the edge
No longer differentiating birdsong trills
No longer reckless with love
No longer in tiresome need of shade
No longer keeping the tally of gold bracelets
Sliding down an aunt's delicate wrists
No longer beholden to tall tales peddled by merciless older cousins
No longer kicking heels
No longer approximating flight
No longer in possession of hilly clearing claimed as sovereign playground
No longer in possession of body
No longer laughing while bleeding at the knees
No longer encrusted with a motherland's red dirt
No longer bypassing chores for rough riot afternoons
No longer forgetting the old songs
No longer having that luxury
No longer attuned to the rupture of spring
No longer long-lashed & unsuspecting
No longer unscathed by canon & caliper
No longer unburdened by the dull weight of philosophy
No longer recognisable to kin
No longer recognisable to self
No longer self, but grasping, huddled, writhing heap of bygones
But no longer

Bankside, Before

What better place than this then could we find,
By this sweet stream that knows not of the sea,
That guesses not the city's misery

— William Morris, 'June'

Once, I was the hull of an empty belly, the belly of an empty hull. Sweat-drenched atrophy. Alone in fevered visions of Akan hands massaging blossom oil into Akan scalps. Flinching at the desertion of touch, I listened to the sound of another boy's murmured distress. He sounded like me, though I couldn't be sure. I sounded like me, though I couldn't be sure. Bruised flesh keeps its inventory of histories, of tactile trails. Reversed. Reverberating. Alone, for what seemed like an unfurling eternity of starless night. The sea owes no allegiances. Elders made their absence known in their proverbs. Below, the bilges groaned like birthing women. Water lapped against time's blunted procession. I sat without speech, as I sat so often, if given the chance, in the brocaded smoking rooms of reclining gentlemen. Before, I knew only of the cloaked fog behind eyelids. Capture swells the vocabulary of abyss. The darkness of the hold. The hold of the darkness. I conversed with a candle's torturous drip. Wordless, I mouthed a shattered count. Onyame! Your son begged. Still awaiting an opening of forked favour. Oracular spirit! Steady these young, hapless feet. Rain-giver, shower us with your sodden blessings. Encircle me with the crush of hailstones, the battering rams of wind & thunder. Tug at your moon. Scrape the tide back from its regular horizons. Don't leave me to my own devices, to their unutterable vices. Help me bear their language of the lash, their lip of horsetail whip. The graveyard floats. There are lessons in the duplicity of waves. I held my tongue. I held onto my tongue.

15

girlchild emblem   exotic gift

borrowed lilt   clutch of pearls

bragging material   household pride

displayed artifact   future keepsake

missing souvenir   breaking the glass

souring the fruit   of their delusions

confinement animates   rippling energy

is sharp ache   of expanding appetite

for birthright   for bread & belonging

dissociated   from self

in fifty words   or less

jostling alongside   shirking soldiers

errant deserters   minor thieves

& wide boy chancers   her reflection an announcement

funhouse mirror   a thoroughbred mare lost

on the same day she ran   the paragraph's span

its solemn width   another arrival

another auction block   each line a threat

of return   freedom is an inconvenience

she hurtles towards   indefinite

Impressment

the local gazette is the garrote is the silver collar is the attached boy of fifteen
       is the girl of twelve the timeline of disguised stealth
       the assumption of rude health of grateful prisoners
       the cruelty is in the detail
       the disappearing of stubborn roots
       the pitiless definition of recovery leaps
       from brooch pinned on breast pocket
       to the crumpled pages of a fitful age
       this register of length between narrow shoulders
       the length of her glaring absence his resplendent audacity
       the daring act of abandon codified in
       daily announcements regular menace
       the common betrayal of identifiers
       creole / negro / east indian / african / native
       intimate interloper
       snatched guest with no return ticket
       noted; the exact shade the sun bestows
       the common charm of crooked teeth
       the mole under his soft chin
       the shy emergence of fuzz
       birthmarks of disregarded origins catalogued beside
       the constellations of smallpox scars
       the mangled cross-link of tissue
       covering her left palm
       their light-fingered hands the listed skills
       the platter the tray the iron the sheets the finery
       dissident domestic servant page boy housegirl property
       each vessel of lofty impressions of genteel nods
       wearing the Venetian red wound of a cravat like a representative
       of family crest of honour of hearth of marching civilisation
       the invisible made visible
       unmistakable in their hunger

Portrait I

bound to periphery

at the brink even when pulled

to silken bosom

to lap doll rehearsals

ribboned light grazes upturned cheek

harsh chiaroscuro

moon-eyed opulence

a beaded waistcoat the colour of a weeping sunrise

ostrich feather arms aloft

peacock splendour

fanning the swooning

pallid foreheads of long-necked mistresses

the boundaries hold steadier than the centre

parameters guarded by fixed orders

steadied by the balance of patronage & bottomless greed

by held poses

by the studied arrangement

of small limbs

pigment dries on fingertips

the table heaves

ringlets escape their braided confines

the prop is beckoned

spills out of the frame

out of velvet crush

into heirloomed wilderness

into the glittering margins of

a narrow frame

Portrait II

Amphibious in my affections, I lick the plate clean.

Besides her lap, I wait. Besides his feet, I furnish

Europe's fantasies. Withdraw from the scene

As swiftly as I enter it.

Embrace or enclosure. Choose what you see.

In one, an opal hangs from my earlobe. In another,

A turban rests atop my still head.

A litter of spaniels pawing at my boots. We reenact the dinner,

The dance, the hunt, the courtly thrum, the necessary lubrication

Of hierarchies. I take my place.

Arm myself with shrouded intentions.

Learn from the indiscriminate surrender of paper to wet brush.

Who can stop the flow of human want?

Who dares stand in its cascading way?

Oil hardens. I answer to my temporary role. Tomorrow,

I smudge the canvas with my disappearance.

Recognition

We meet again, without fanfare.
Street names introduce us to ourselves.
The Blackamoor's Head, Blackamoor Alley, Black Boy Court.
In this reflection, we are distorted.
Our faces reveal the gashes of our separation.
Dahomey, Ardra, Antigua, Spanish Town.
We name this lonely truth: freedom. It crouches between us,
Shaky-legged & newborn.

Some run with it, this freedom of scraps & damp alleyways.
They cluster in the dark,
Dot the city with their clutched need.
The profane mewling of hungry children. The youngest stare
Blankly, wide eyes like milk saucers. It is too hard to look.
Harder still, to look away.
Too much between us, too much has torn us
Away from the unforgiving commonality of origins.
We know each other by names we did not choose for ourselves.

Is the price of freedom a bed in an airless room?
A meal scraped from the bottom of the burnt pan?
Is it the gasp of air on a morning outing? The stolen moments
Of quiet conversation with another?
Who stands closer to the clenched hand?
Who sleeps with an empty belly?
Who walks in rags but laughs without shame, with their shivering own?

GBOYEGA ODUBANJO

A Negro Boy named Goude, aged about 17, speaks no English, Run away on Sunday last at Six in the Evening, had on an old sad-coloured serge Coat, a pair of sad-coloured cotton Breeches, and an old black Tarrey Hat on his head. Whoever brings him to Lyme-house, to Mr John Woodfine, shall have Forty shillings Reward.

— The London Gazette, 23rd December 1686

In the resources, as well as in conversations with Dr. Peggy Brunache, I came across some evidence of community amongst the enslaved people, however such evidence was scarce. In contrast to the experiences of enslaved people in the Americas and Caribbean, where on a daily basis one is surrounded by others in the same conditions as themselves, slavery in the UK seemed to be relatively solitary. As such, I tried to explore possible connections that reframed the narratives so the people within were less isolated—literally, figuratively, conceptually, in language, etc. I think some of these attempts were more successful than others. The connections that I explored were to traditions of pre-colonial Yorubaland, the language and rhythms of braggadocious and luxury rap, the idea of a house party in East London, and family across the diaspora.

As I went about this, my biggest challenge was in trying to avoid reproducing, through language, the violence done to enslaved people. There is a degree of risk in trying to problematise already problematic language and I am grateful to Fahad Al-Amoudi for challenging me to think more deeply about the ways in which I was trying to parody the resource texts.

Finally, much of my work prior to this project has focused on the significance of naming. The absence of names in the vast majority of newspaper adverts as well as the list of names in church records particularly stood out to me. These acts of un-naming (through descriptors such as 'black woman', as well as the Anglicisation or replacement of names) aid not only in the dehumanisation of enslaved people but also in the erasure of their histories and cultures. Where appropriate, I wanted to foreground the names I found in the resources and acknowledge the power inherent within them. Elsewhere, I wanted to highlight the discomfort that arises when people are reduced to mere descriptors.

Classified

we do not know the name   black boy   aged twelve   well-set
with a good grasp of english   has run   described as agreeable
no vices the young   fellow believed to be between eleven
and fifteen has been reported   missing from listed address
in the west   london area   physical description states   child
is well-proportioned wooly   hair close to head like crown   if anyone
is to apprehend the fourteen-year-old and return them a reward
twenty shillings   breaking   vanished has a west african   black
said to struggle   with the tongue full eyes   all yellow
aged about seventeen   heading eastward wanting   of some toes   a plea
lookout for indian black diamonds   at their temples   hair curled like the rest
three guineas for capture   child still maturing   we have been informed
clothed in drugget gown   dark cinnamon hat   public warned   be vigilant
evil visible in her neck   if approached by aforementioned   black of adult age
this woman   in the whitechapel area   still wanting toes   and front teeth
if she appears wanting of a name refusing   english if she has   a mark
on her   face belonging to her country itself wanting   of a name   forehead
resembling flower   blooming heading eastward still   escort back   forty shillings

Grave Goods

We do not know exactly, but there exists the possibility that, as Goude's life shrunk into history, he remained stuck in place. Yes, his body moved—from embrace to hold. And he may not have known, but yes, the water moved—from coast to arid coast. But perhaps, when he looked into the face of the man who claimed him, Goude saw just another Benin City chief with more wanting than there was to have. Except, in this man, Goude saw what he had known to be the signs of death—spirit alive, lips thin as a procession. And who's to say Goude didn't then see himself—practicing out the steps he would take to follow this man into the ground. Maybe Goude saw people with whom he shared only one thing—oblations to wealth—praying their own last rites—lowered to dirt—ready to serve owner and owner's owner in the next world and the next's next. It is difficult to imagine that Goude would have needed to see any more than this. It is easy enough to see him returning to the ocean—hoping that on the other side—whatever direction—he might live to die a death wholly his own.

Proprietor Rap

might just spend a boy on a necklace
sell a boy for a pipe of madeira   come
by him   come and buy a boy split
the booty spin the yarn take the boy
as gospel   my assets have assets
my boy has the painted-callico
with the buttons   call him a steal
swallow hook line and   haggle
over his days his particulars
the background of my paintings
have lives of their own   that's
my father's name on the collar
that's the blue waistcoat with
the matching stockings   might just
cop nab drop a pretty penny
on a boy of such as shall happen
to die   call me mister mister   nothing
that i can't have   my collection
looking like a registrar   put a house
on a boy   put him on a boat somewhere
no-one can find   grease his palms
send the boy off for a song   get me another

social death is a house party for smart people – **Fred Moten**

what we do know or can surmise is that in the summer of 1764

there appears to have been what we might today call a motive

you know the vibes

no less than sixty in the place in the city there is a place

beyond sight and hearing

call it the mobility inside the immobility

subjugation is a loose snare if you've got the hips

if your name ain't on the list just say where you stay at

where you running to little man

say hello to jean and mary gray everybody knows sabinah

careful of king aka john king that man a mischief

give him a string and he'll pull you a mile east

give him a few more he'll fiddle a sound to escape to

don't mind cudjoe quaco bembo lothario

peter behaves as well as you can expect

you see a man name himself thomas clarke just know

he means fortune and if he's a christian

then i've got a mansion and a road with your name on it

come get stupid come get deluded away

take you down black boy alley show you

where the ppldem stay under the bridges

bottom of the tankard you'll find a spot

show you a spot to claim you welcome

to the united kingdom of not here let me

take your jacket and fix you something

Cousin

dear cousin how are you over
on that side. i hear you lot get
a bit of sun and field. does the
heat cling. we don't get much
on this side. i'm not sure
if you get much smog. sometimes
it looks like there's more of us
than there are but then it rains
like it's rainy season. everything
is grey-shaped. is it true you have
barrels just for laughing.
i've stopped talking. the one fella
i knew got on a boat. lucky bastard
wasn't even happy. said he was going
to die. what is dying if not this. cousin
i know you've got your family.
i don't want to impose. if you could write.
tell me is there a space for me there.
i hope this reaches you somehow
because i can find a way—warmly

cousin. i pray this finds its way to you.
my mum still talks about how we used
to run around in the rain chasing chickens.
don't think i've been clean like that since.
i saw a painting—the way you lot look
over on your side—boy don't you boys
wash up good. had me thinking black
was white for a second. i joke but i like
to picture you going on strolls with the king
in your frocks and your waistcoats
speaking your la di da. everytime i hear one
of them ships have come i wait to see if it's you.
but those who come always look so broken.
here everything up to our tongue is breaking.
if you get this please write. and maybe soon
we might see each other again. maybe we
meet somewhere in the middle of this. yours—

TASIA GRAHAM

Run away from her Mistress, last Saturday Morning, a young Negro Woman, about 15 Years old. She has a remarkable large Cut over each of her Cheeks, being her Country Mark in Guinea, is marked on the left Shoulder E.P. speaks English very indifferently, is short of stature, and had on when she went away, a Stuff Black and White Cross-barr'd Gown, Check'd Apron, Handkerchief and Petticoat, Red Cloak and Black Silk Hat; and stole two silver Spoons mark'd in a Cypher M G.

Whoever will give Information of her, so that she may be got again, shall receive a Reward of Five Guineas, by applying at the Bar of the Jamaica Coffee-house in St. Michael's Alley, Cornhill; and if the Spoons are offered for Sale or Pawn, please to stop them and the Party, and give Notice to Sir John Fielding, and you shall receive the same Reward.

— The Public Advertiser, 6th November 1764

In my illustrations, I wanted to show the life of someone before being shipped to London—their history, journey and identity, during and after being enslaved. In order to realise the concept, it was important for me to depict the daily lives of enslaved people in Britain.

During my research I found that they were given mundane tasks, such as washing, cleaning, shopping and wore clothes given by their masters. I illustrated an enslaved Black woman, running through the streets of London, and then finding herself back in the hands of her master, having to relive the same thing over again. Then, after many years, she gains her own freedom, shown in the third illustration.

As she sits in the chair, you can see her former self behind her, her African culture on the right and her enslaved self on the left. She now has to face the idea that she may be Black-British, but she is not viewed as a citizen due to the colour of her skin, nor does she identify with the culture she once had. This illustration depicts the confusion and the loss of African identity, that many Black-British people face today with a loss in their culture and who they really are, through the effects of slavery.

Forgotten journey of the enslaved

© Tasia Graham

Escaped, captured and repeated

© Tasia Graham

British, with a loss of identity

© Tasia Graham

OLUWASEUN OLAYIWOLA

A Negro, and 5 Guineas Reward

Absented from his Master in Craven Street, in the Strand, on the 5th Instant, a Negro Fellow, named Cato; who was christened at St Giles's, on the 23rd April last, by the Name of John Rowland. He is supposed to be upwards of 20 Years of Age, and not exceeding five Feet three Inches high, being of a very small Size, but with an old and grave look. He reads, writes and speaks English pretty well, plays on the Violin, dresses Hair, and is well known in and about York Buildings. When he absconded he had on a green Coat, with a red Velvet Collar, and white Metal Buttons. As he may offer his Service to some Gentlemen, it is hoped they will not afford him any Encouragement; and whoever gives Information (so that he may be secured by his Master) to Mr. Blamire, Stationer, the Corner of Craven Street aforesaid, shall receive Five Guineas Reward.

N.B. If he returns of his own Accord, he shall be received and his Misbehaviour will be overlooked; otherwise every Means will be used to discover and apprehend him: And whoever harbours and entertains him, will be prosecuted with the utmost severity of the Law.

— The Public Advertiser, 26th June 1771

It feels natural to me to write about desire. What felt unnatural was to write about desire rising from silence, from an incompleteness, like seeing black smoke pluming in the distance yet being unable to identify exactly what caught fire.

I tried various methods: inundating myself with the archival material, gathering images as if they were data, even erasing some of the provided material to see what hidden codes and beauty were already camouflaged in the language. The resulting poems from these methods felt accurate but not precise. Put another way, they seemed to reflect what was already known. They choked mystery, leading them to an inertness that lacked, in my view, emotional authority. I had to recover my initial curiosity about the research which, not surprisingly, brought me back to a question I am often contending with myself: what is it like to have a body?

Yet, in one sense, the archive was structured as a sort of body; albeit a body with gaps, negative spaces, paginated caverns. A productive tension then arose in my thinking about the runaways: the predicament of having been in a body – physically, communally – while simultaneously being absent from one – legally, metaphysically, and archivally. We know they existed because there are small hard-to-read generalizations about their features, clothes, and their fitness for labor at the time of their disappearance.

It was hard to write these poems, to think that my voice, emerging as it is, filled with its own obsessions and blindspots, could even tangentially intimate the lives of these freedom-seekers. I hope these poems contain even a fraction of the complexity and bravery I understand their lives to have exemplified. If at all they do, they are the beginning of a needed, continuous honoring.

Dark and Peculiar Case

It's his logic that's backwards: he pours into me
what he cannot forget. Every Tuesday night
he enters the bushes, throws his clothes
into a pile on mine, then waits.

It's like he's waiting for himself to stop himself.

Even the silence waits, opened between us
like a wound rejecting its scab.
This isn't unbearable.
It's the breaking into another man's body,
it's the being broken into—

I know his two faces: pleasure and disgust.
Trying to distinguish them is like looking
at the river's surface: it depends
what shimmers at the top in moonlight.

Look away briefly and it's gone.
If you see his, you certainly cannot see mine.

Blood in the blueblossoms
but this is not the odor rousing nausea
in the atmosphere of his desire, his God-given right.

But the law here is God: it must
be interpreted, must have context.
Tonight my body is his vigil,
as if his mind were sleepwalking.

Tomorrow, we both wake up in a changed body,
the scab like a weed lacerated above ground,
the root deepening its secret in the earth.

Don't believe me?
Look around you and smell the air.

My heart goes flaccid, week
after week after week—

It is he who thinks he is like any man,
who forgets in the dark, he too
is penetrable.

Epistemology

Then the blue moons
of my legs pedaling
alleyways in whispers.

Not night, not
utterly yet — rickets
of rubbish under the mist,
how far to go when to go
nowhere is far enough?

Race—where does the line finish
versus curl into the body's opened-wide-
by-force room, now made loud, now dangerous,
now running tracks in the grass like a letter
you regret sending—little taint of stars
illuminating this tamed geography.
This running is for everyone

who is not running, who got caught inside themselves
like a thief, community of bone and skin and bread
and misfire and want and the mist, once rising, plateauing
into what is economic, breathable

which does not mean safe, does not mean granted
by the law, not for those who look like me, not for those moved in
and by the shadowed world of white and fearful giants—is it you
who can escape, is it me restricted to images—these trees,

these ivies, these birds, will they remember? These humans,
will they try? This light my body is coming more quickly into
like kindling. You are not trained to see where the burn began. Blank

encyclopedia. Field of gone-stars. Gestured sky. Ghosts filling-in where sky ends so it never
ends, in the belly of it where the divide disappears. Go ahead. Ask what you should know
already of the streets, the squares, circuses, bricks, everywhere there is not a voice, everywhere
music tucks a time past into the faculties, the blazed hole of three guineas in the pocket.

What is the reward that you want? Tell me about you. What is missing from you? Did you love? Did you twist? Did you cheat? Did you revise your body back to your own property? Why do you think you belong to your body? Repetition is a pattern the body remembers to forget. How far will I go into this forgetting? Not far. Nowhere here is far enough.

Stay there in this nowhere you are gliding in, where all will convince you we are not already fused—but fused into what?

You are not far from it. You are exactly where it is supposed to be beginning. You are doing nothing.

Yet I want to be my own person, to be my own I. I cannot stand here in this ink.

That you think 'I' is alive in these shallowing lines.

So concerned with the *why*?

Who does the question blow towards and when?

Who does the question blow behind like a tailwind—

Blank encyclopedias.

Fields of gone-stars.

Ghosts filling-in

where *why?* ends

so it never ends

Love Poem from the Underworld

And it was as it had always been, difference
between moving in
and moving from shadow, barely, atleast I thought,
discernable, saintliness,
as is the way in moral tales, scattering
the sun into unchanged stars, still-light, still light.

The pang of the gavel jamming the wood,
earned emission on the blackest face, that meant
we had assaulted each other's bodies
according to the courts.
Court—funny word.
Is that not why I was *sitting* on him?

Is that not why we flipped our names:
Thrust. Ache. Thrust. Ache.
A little wind, a little gin
splattering like target practice.
Token. Bounty. To whom
shall I speak tonight,

in this assumption of starlight,
this shiver congealing
at the gossamered edge
of the skin, simultaneously
mine and not mine. Is it you, love,
that I steal this body for? You

who calls me *dear,* calls me *precious,*
honest, calls me *anything*
but free. My face only partly visible now,
as if it were coming through cloudwork, as if
my hands around his neck like shackles,
my fingers down the bony islands of his spine—

His body, a violence of love, in mine. I
consent, I thrust and ache, thrust
and ache for my shadow life.
How do you build a home
in another man's body with no manual?
As is the way in moral tales—he was wrong,

that judge. This was not attempted
sodomy. Daybreak was coming
so light and groan
fused in one trapped sound, barely
discernable. All we had left was this context.
On Sodomite's Walk we ran for our lives—

Once

That brief and grief rhyme is the irony, forever
opening black-handed waves like reveries

in the water. Folding—grabbing. Enough
actionless bodies floating in the ocean

and it becomes one, black buoyancies
organizing like a wet calligraphy—

shipwood. Compasses. The aftereffect
of grief—still grief? Dark islands

expanding abyssward, as when solitude tips
into loneliness and only the darkest

seabirds lift their wings into the sky's empty sigh,
a hush of escape's distress signal dripping

off their flanks like flares, as if you could locate
the difference between memory and freedom,

the darkest seabirds now flying overhead
in a flock as I run through the hedges—

you tell me what could bring them back to the beginning
of this blue maneuver of dream? O to be inside that flight,

to be damaged beyond the instinct of return—

ABENA ESSAH

Whereas a black Negro Woman, about nineteen Years old, with two Letters on her Breast and Shoulder, made her Escape out of the Ship Hannah, Capt. Fowler, for Jamaica, the 6th of June last, goes by the Name of Sabinah, is supposed to be deluded away by some other Blacks about Whitechapel, Rag-Fair, or Rotherhith: Whoever brings her to the late Mr. Neate's, on Lawrence-Pountney-Hill, shall have Three Guineas Reward.

— The Daily Advertiser, 14th September 1743

The reality of community, the preservation of indigenous culture and the intertwining lives of the enslaved people who sought out freedom, were the main themes that underpinned my poems. As a child of the Ghanaian Diaspora, I was brought up knowing that community is integral to Ghanaian and Black culture and so this was essential to explore. Sabinah was one of the people that stood out to me for this reason; I was struck by the fact that she had been 'deluded away by some blacks'. I imagined those who were enslaved going about their 'Master's business' and meeting other Black people who they would talk to and dream with. I also thought a lot about the intimacy of the Black community in London and how likely it was that the lives of freedom-seekers would intertwine.

It was also important to address the fact that freedom-seekers were traumatised by the violence of enslavement and how this violence is mapped onto the modern-day realities for Black communities in London. I was particularly drawn to the map that compared old and modern East London for that reason. I also wanted to explore the role of the Church, Christianity and colourism as I am aware of the huge role of these systems in chattel slavery.

Moreover, as a queer non-binary person it was important for me to queer up the research. Precolonial queer ancestry is rich within the African continent and this fact should be widely known. Thus, telling a queer love story between two people of Ghanaian and Nigerian heritage not only gave me the chance to explore indigenous cultures and religions but it also allowed me to explore the truth – that queerness was and is a beautiful and common reality within the African continent.

Escape Route

Mile End, 23rd December 1686

My Kwabena's lips are warm
his back against the brick

gold glow pulsing from the Ball
outlines the full of his bottom lip,

muffled music, black folk and
swing dancing keep us company,

hand tracing his neck
like that day thigh to thigh in March

teaching his hands to stretch to my native God
Olodumare; Ashe flows endless within us

our bodies, formless and fluid
limbs hot, our beards meshing

Kwabena recalled his Maame lifting and
pounding bankye and brodeɛ

fufuo steaming with fish and soup
his hands scouping mouthful after mouthful.

Now he pulls at my tongue with his teeth sharp
I can tell when he remembers, a hunger to his pace;

the purpling of his skin, the pounding
siblings screaming at sea, thrown overboard.

Now, I wrap my arms around the future of him
'The whole of London will be looking for you Tobi'

he is whispering, like that first day at the piers
his hand, grabbing my leg in the shadow

of the street corner; my arms are hauling
crates of Woodfine's food,

brass choking my throat.
Kwabena had known them once

the routes I dragged my body along
so he never looked away.

Here cheek to cheek we know,
we cannot give each other our Mother's back

our tongues do not fold the same syllables
but we can name each other

Goude to Oluwatobi
Unnamed to Akan

Woodfine cannot find us here.

Sunday Service

For Matt, Jane and Maria

An unusually large number of people who were described as 'Black' appear in [St Margaret's Church's] baptismal records... Clearly the church was welcoming to them, whether enslaved or free. The rector at that time was Thomas Wilson, but no evidence survives to explain why he and his church were so welcoming to this particular community.

— Simon P. Newman

1719: My blotchy torso swings
from the window yelling jump,
Father knows I will survive a fall this high,
bolts it every night.
Bolts my mouth.
But I found the key,
I miss my mother
reaching from Maryland
cupping my face
so warm, I jump!
Hear her screaming
the night father ripped me from her.
She always said 'Matt look for God when you
lose the weight of your father. Look for God.'

1758: I pull my robe over my head
it never gets old,
how my curls jump up against the fabric.
The clergy are flooding
black and humming last sermon's hymns,
I head to the altar
to lead,
my eyes no longer closed to their suffering.

1719: God is sitting
on the altar when I arrive;
glass stains my beige skin
orange and fuchsia.
A white man is reading to God.
My shoulders scrunch,
he beckons me.
I want to lose my father.
But God beckons me too
and Mother whispers go;
my shoulders drop.

White man in white robe
teaches my limbs to rest,
Teaches my beige body to fathom thirty years from now.
Straightens my curls,
teaches my skin to pass,
teaches my eyes to close to black suffering,
under the church
screaming the way mother did.
At the piers, under ships
on the street corners
their hands cupped begging.
I pray to God
To rest. To lose my father.

1758: 'I Rector Wilson, baptise you
Jane and Maria Grey in the name of the father,
of the ones we have lost and to the ones who will sing'.
I shed fountains of water from my eyes
it happens every time.
Stain glass light is spilling on me,
beige skin is orange and fuchsia again;
the clergy is swelling with pigment and gospel,
my mother reaches down from the blue above St Paul's
her pride warm on my cheeks;
I have lost the weight of my father.

Keep Breathing

Woodfine: Have you spilt the wine again?

Negro:

Woodfine: What do you have to say for yourself *****?

Negro:

He is pounding. Black flesh is hard to discolour. I am purpling. The velvet will need washing.
The wine was poured not spilt. Mepε sε mekɔ fie. My mouth lets out shrill screaming.

I recoil into my brain. Ohene Obiri Yeboah appears from the thick fog. Our people, hands
sturdy march forward, his throne resting upon their shoulders. Heavy gold cuddles his
fingers;
sun yellow fabric with scarlet squares is draping Ohene's shoulder. The clanging of
dawuro begins. The lifting of curved stick to drum skin. Curved stick to drum. Stick to
drum. To drum.

Everything hurts.

Our people are a mirror of me, arms, legs tucking and bending, dancing the Adowa
again.
I lift and tuck, tuck, lift, arching my back.

Breathe, breathe.

Sturdy hands lower the throne, swaying skirts brushing the ground. Ohene stands on
orange soil with us. Calabash brimming with palm wine. 'Nananom nsamanfoɔ monεgye
nsa'. We pour palm wine. 'Nananom nsamanfoɔ mommɔ Kwabena ho ban'. We pour
palm wine. The dead are breathing among us; the dead are breathing among us

Woodfine: Next time I won't be so sparing *****

Kwabena: *(legs convulsing)*

Me dwane wonnhu me bio. Mekɔ fie. I can fit through the gap in the window. My mind is so foggy. At the
piers some boys - eyes mahogany like Ohene showed me their blue veins and smiles told me, my blood too
will stay blue if I run

Nothing's Changed

I burst out of Starbucks panting,
he didn't see me.
Cars on the main road, shooting by.
I pull the sad coloured velvet
above my neck
to cover my dog collar
embossed with the address for my execution.

At Liverpool Street Station,
Ragfair market
is bustling, white men
selling and stealing
second hand shoes and breeches.
I take cover
free negros in the corner of the fair,
they sell garments our fathers used to wear
at our ceremonies of celebration.

I can hear them shouting for me now
'Has anyone seen a Negro boy run?'

The train leaves
2 minutes
I remember
board

Another white man
Has his eyes
Trained on me
My skin can't hide
Cold sweats

*

I was told to head North,
peering outside the bus window
Black boys spilling
onto pavements
clanging hollow penny tins

'230 to Upper Walthamstow'

All of London's buses are red

'Black Boy Lane'

The flag's lion is red
blood has a funny way of spilling

A black boy's eye
catches mine,
I bolt off the bus

On this road
We all stay low
Hush hush
Face heavy with death
And black boy spirit
We are trying

        *

Is it St Paul's Cathedral or is it St Margaret's Church?
An aunty, hands clutched, knees pressed to the pew
tells me she came for Rector Wilson,
for the black service,
for holy water, for a better life.
White men look for her sons
to this day.
The newspapers
calling for auction:
NEGRO BOY RAN AWAY FROM HIS MASTER
Whoever should bring him back
shall be rewarded with three guineas.
Tall and sturdy negro boy.
Black male with a history of violence.
Call the metropolitan police
if you see this dangerous suspect

          *

Hush, hush, black boy, don't let them catch you slipping

Bra Fie

For Sabinah

Homecoming Ball, Rotherhithe, 18th June 1743

Song of brass horns
is rich dancing through my scalp;
he shaved my coils but they are growing. Black
hands, black hands grasping music; black eyes are
wide eyed, I rest my eyelids. Listen to the swell of thudding
drum beating, beating. We are so many, grinning teeth, tightly packed
but upright; yellow glow kissing the cheeks of everything. A man gets up to
swirl, shoulder blades bending, hands lifted - ghost of orange soil flicking at his feet.
Blood
congeals on his back, raw wounds from whipping. He keeps swirling. Red still dripping

red in my mouth.
Back cold on ship Hannah's floor
metal heaving my windpipe
brothers' limbs on top of me
feet in my mouth.

They came to get me: Shaquan, Oluwafemi, Afia. He tried to pack me away, chains again but
they gripped me with hands so warm, in cunning Navy sailor suits, telling white men on deck
'Mr Neate's request: Sabinah is needed up stream'
Goodbye death in Jamaica.
In this room we are the sun's offspring. Elder Oppong glides to the centre, dancing
scatters; he calls the names of us, fresh arrivals: 'James Asante, Anike Yahaya
Akosua Darkwah'
Akosua, the name Sunday sung for me
out the womb, I arise. Women who know the weight of me approach
speaking the language my spine was bent to forget,
resting wise palms upon my shoulders;
diaphragms swelling

Nyame yɛda woase
Me Nyankopɔn yɛyi woayɛ
Sɛ wode Akosua abeduru asumdwiem
Yɛnnsu bio
Ɛmom yɛbɛ sa na yɛagye yen ani
Odomankoma yɛda woase

Densu river is streaming down my cheeks

the letters on my shoulder

peel in the warmth of it all

OLIVIA TWIST

Ran away, a Young Negro Fellow, named Othello, about nineteen Years of Age, stout and well made, speaks good English, had on when he went away, a light Cloth Coat, turn'd up with blue Cuffs and Collar, lined with Blue, plain white Metal Buttons, blue Cloth Waistcoat, with blue and white Lace, Doeskin Breeches, ribb'd Worsted Stockings, Silver Buckles in his Shoes and Knees, and an old Silver-laced Hat; the said Negro was christened some Time ago at London-Stone Church, by the name of Robert Ward. If he will return home (as those, who, It's imagined, corrupted him, are removed) his past Faults will be forgiven; if not, whoever will give Information to Mr James Concanen, in Bell-Yard, opposite the Monument, so that he may be secured, shall have a reward of Four Guineas. The above Negro had with him a French Horn, on which he was learning to play.

— The Daily Advertiser, 28th January 1761

Anyone who knows me knows how I love to make noise about how much I love anything to do with East London and that love just got a whole lot deeper during this research process. The size of the Black population in East London all those hundreds of years ago was strong. Resistance can take the form of rest and finding love. It's been happening here on our door step. The locality of it all is really the thing that we have to highlight. It happened near where we would go to buy school uniforms all them years ago. It happened where we go and picnic when it's proper hot. It happened all over the areas we used to go and drop off our CVs in the hopes of bagging that first weekend job. Time and time again we are reminded of how we seem to have a knack for finding the small glimmer of joy, and fanning that.

Black Owned Taverns

© Olivia Twist

Blooming Communities in the East

© Olivia Twist

Finding Love in Billingsgate Market

© Olivia Twist

MEMOONA ZAHID

An Indian black Girl, aged about 15, with a Brass Collar about her Neck, in a Drugget Gown and a Painted-Callico Petticoat, Run away from Captain John Bowers in Rotherhith, on Monday night last. Whoever brings her to Captain Bowers aforesaid, shall have a Guinea Reward, and Charges.

— The London Gazette, 22nd September 1690

The research that I felt drawn to immediately was the newspaper advertisement of the unnamed 15-year-old South Asian girl who escaped from her enslavement in Rotherhithe. The advert specifies the clothing 'painted-callico' and a brass collar around her neck, and I wanted to write from this perspective because I immediately had a vision of her running – and I felt a prayer surge inside me for her; that she would find her community and be safe.

Writing this poem meant searching deeply within myself as well as into the research. In her collection *Look*, Solmaz Sharif writes 'It matters what you call a thing'. Reading about the people who escaped from enslavement, I realised I didn't know their lives, their names, their joys, or friendships. Naming the people in this poem was a way for me to begin to uncover and write into the possibility of their lives. The title of my poem refers to that possibility, the possibility of entering the poem, which is one interpretation, and the re-imagining of a life.

It was important for me to find and present beauty in the poem – I felt the bleakness of history and how its impact underlines and shapes our existences, and whilst there are moments in the poem where this is acute, I hope to have shown some of the variousness of life too.

A possible entrance into the moon

she sneaks lavender from the gardens

            slips it   under her pillow

drowsiness opens inside her

           & fear

festers in her limbs but she sleeps

          & refuses the sound of the moon

          refuses the blisters on her palms

          the same shape of ba's eyes

refuses the call of sunrise

refuses her stomach

        its eternal presence like the wind humming against hanging clothes

fear opens a fist at her neck

     sickness is her only reprieve –

              she imagines her sleep

                becoming a grave

the soil littered with a field of fallen winter honey suckle

        not ma or ba surrounding her

        but gallons of soundless earth

            ;

    every beginning is a middle so she begins

    open   down her middle

                                    a throat

                                    torn apart

                                    overripe apple

on the roof of her mouth   she remembers the name ba gave her

        a mouth knows the shape of a word even when it's left unsaid

                        for years

                        her tongue traces   back & forth over her front teeth

        she's waited to say it aloud   only now

        like a bird   escaping its aviary

        does she dare –

                Pari

                                    ;

        whilst ripping out blades of grass she prayed –

                around her neck the brass weighed like a promise

ready to be broken

                the sky   a whirlpool spinning out god's answer:

                                    Run

                            Layla devised

        the plan

        hair tied up

        sleeves rolled up

her face

like Moses after emerging from the ocean

in the other house

Layla's fingers bled   each bandage wound tight

suspended circulation

like a single uprooted sycamore tree

sometimes   after the length of the day has sunk into them

like feet stood in an overgrown field

they hold their hands up against the sky

& smile

to be alive is to feel

& the whole sun weaves through their fingers onto their faces

;

Pari's spent a lifetime waiting   wanting

for tenderness to spring up like cygnets emerging

she runs until she reaches

a possible

entrance

into the moon

empty of belongings

she only carries herself

& her memories

her petticoats   the colour of Rotherhithe

vines growing up concrete buildings

ensnaring

the path from her feet to her waist

rainwater slapping her ankles

her skirts drenched

a half-lit pavement

half a moth glides on to her palm

ba's words chant through her being

when you find emptiness

stay a while

remember the smell of tangerines

how each is one made by god just for you

;

she had tried to escape once before

she wanted to disappear

dreams of her evergreen face

evaporating into fog

came to her like flying ants

suddenly everywhere

;

cold

her teeth loud   rain-like

the ceiling touches the tip of her head

a spider web against her eye

72

a fly hissing as the spider crawled

the world is an eye

                          it watches as she wanders through

            the movement of her limbs

the inside of her arms

                grey like the wings of the fly

                    the eye watches her mind as it forgets the shape

of the bones in ma's face

      days after   her hands cradle her knees

                          she yearns to belong to something light

                          her idea of heaven

                          or somewhere warm somewhere

                          with summer rain & Layla's voice

               ;

she had not expected this

           her people with their arms speaking into other arms

                          the lull of their voices

                          in beat with the drums

      the afterglow of a heavy sunset as it swims into the walls

      the smell of bread

                    her mouth a child again

                    her mouth allowed to be a child again

she knows she's loved like this before   unrelenting

like cherries   cold against her forehead her cheeks

        she swallows seed after seed
        ripping apart the fruit with her teeth
              savouring the ache in her throat as she beckons

            a forest
               to replace her physical being

                  ;

Layla is nowhere

              inside her eardrum
              an echo
              like the inside of a shell

                  lost

                 ;

            Pari casts her eyes over the river
instead of trembling water she sees
a crowd of faces like her own

               mouths wide & wailing
               the same song

among them ba & ma   floating up to the scintillating deep sun
                 the way the angels had gone
            into a lavender infused sleep

GLOSSARY & NOTES

Introduction *Page 9*

enslaved… indigenous Americans: While there are records of a small number of indigenous people from the Americas being enslaved in London during this period, there is no evidence of their escaping although these attempts, successful or not, would certainly have been made.

'Bankside, Before' *Page 15*

Onyame: or 'Nyame' is the Akan/Twi word for God and refers specifically to an omniscient and omnipotent god.

'Impressment' *Page 17*

silver collar: On Middle Passage ships and on plantations in the colonies the enslaved wore cast iron shackles, but in London enslaved personal servants were often adorned with brass or silver collars. These expensive restraints were intended to advertise masters' wealth and on occasion a master's name and address were engraved on the collar.

birthmarks of disregarded origins: One way to determine if someone was of African or Caribbean descent was whether they were described as having a 'country marks' or scars, ritualised scarification of the faces, arms and torsos of young Africans. This could identify that an enslaved person was from the African continent rather than from the Americas where these practices were not continued.

'Classified' *Page 23*

drugget: a heavy, course, woven woollen fabric.

'Grave Goods' *Page 24*

Benin City: The Kingdom of Benin was an Empire that existed in what is now known as the Edo region of Southern Nigeria. It lasted from around the 11th century until 1897 and at its height, it dominated trade from the Western Niger Delta to modern-day Accra. Today, Benin City is the capital of the Edo region.

'Proprietor Rap' *Page 25*

pipe of madeira: a pipe or 'butt' of madeira was a unit of measurement that referred to 126 gallons of Madeira wine.

painted-callico: brightly-coloured, printed Indian cotton.

as shall happen to die: This phrase comes directly from a Royal African Company report describing a journey Thomas Woodfine's ship took to Jamaica during which 140 enslaved people died.

'Escape Route' *Page 49*

Maame (Twi): Mother

Bankye (Twi): Cassava

Brodeε (Twi): Green Plantain

Fufuo (Twi): Staple traditional Ghanaian food

Olodumare (Yoruba): Yoruba God, omnipotent being who is genderless/possesses all gender identities simultaneously

Ashe (Yoruba): the divine energy that brings all things into existence in Yoruba religion and allows for the potential of Olodumare's infinite iterations

'Sunday Service' *Page 51*

described as 'Black': In many advertisements and baptismal and other records, people of South Asian as well as African descent were described in this way.

'Keep Breathing' *Page 53*

John & Thomas Woodfine: John Woodfine and his brother, Thomas, were slave-traders who captained ships as employees of the Royal African Company. In Abena's poems, the surname 'Woodfine' is a reference to these real-life figures but also an extended metaphor representing the larger oppressive force of slavery.

Mepɛ sɛ mekɔ fie (Twi): I want to go home

Ohene Obiri Yeboah (Twi): Monarch Obiri Yeboah

Dawuro (Twi): Traditional Ghanaian instruments – bells used for the Adowa dance or to announce an important event in traditional Ghanaian culture

Adowa (Twi): Ghanaian Traditional Dance – normally danced at celebrations

Calabash (Twi): Ghanaian traditional cup for drinking and eating

Nananom nsamanfoɔ monɛgye nsa (Twi): the spirit of the Ancestors, hear us as we speak, this is some wine for you.

Nananom nsamanfoɔ mommɔ Kwabena ho ban (Twi): Ancestors of the past, look after and protect Kwabena.

Me dwane wonnhu me bio. Mekɔ fie (Twi): I'm running away, you won't see me ever again, I'm going home.

'Bra Fie' *Page 56*

Bra Fie (Twi): Come home

Nyame yɛda woase (Twi): God we thank you

Me Nyankopɔn yɛyi woayɛ (Twi): My God we praise you

Sɛ wode Akosua abeduru asumdwiem (Twi): For safely and peacefully bringing Akosua back

Yɛnnsu bio (Twi): We won't cry anymore

Ɛmom yɛbɛ sa na yɛagye yen ani (Twi): Instead, we will dance and celebrate

Odomankoma yɛda woase (Twi): God almighty we thank you

BIOS

Momtaza Mehri is a poet and essayist. Her work has appeared in the likes of *Granta, Artforum, The Guardian, BOMB Magazine* and *The Poetry Review*. She is the former Young People's Laureate for London and columnist-in-residence at the San Francisco Museum of Modern Art's Open Space, as well as a Frontier-Antioch Fellow at Antioch University.

Gboyega Odubanjo was born and raised in East London. He is the author of two poetry pamphlets, *While I Yet Live* (Bad Betty Press, 2019) and *Aunty Uncle Poems* (The Poetry Business, 2021). Gboyega is an editor of *bath magg*.

Tasia Graham explores bold, atmospheric, narrative illustration, using her colourful palette and fluid, stylised drawing techniques. Working in both digital format and traditional painting, Tasia explores womanhood, culture, and identity, depicting moods and scenes formed into illustrative storytelling. Tasia draws inspiration from real life experiences and people to create authentic storytelling art.

Oluwaseun Olayiwola is a Nigerian-American dancer, choreographer, poet, and critic based in London. He recently completed an MFA in Choreography from the Trinity Laban Conservatoire of Music in Dance. In 2018, he was awarded a Fulbright Scholarship to study in the United Kingdom. His poems have been published by the Tate, *bath magg, Odd Magazine, Queerlings, VS the Podcast* and *Poached Hare*.

Abena Essah is a multidisciplinary artist based in London. Their work intertwines queer identity, blackness, music and Ghanaian heritage. More recently, their practise has focused on excavating untold stories of Queer African ancestry and Black history. They are a BBC Words First finalist 2020, a Some-Antics Slam Champion and Roundhouse Poetry Slam finalist. Abena Essah is also an alumnus of Obsidian and The Writing Room and has been published in the *Roundhouse Poetry Collective Alumnus Anthology*.

Olivia Twist is an Illustrator, Arts Facilitator and Lecturer from east London with an MA in Visual Communication from the Royal College of Art. The key threads which can be found in her work are place, the mundane and overlooked narratives. She has a strong interest in participatory design, relational aesthetics and documenting social history as it unfolds. As a practitioner her aims are to provide her audience with 'the shock of the familiar' and to trigger greater intergenerational discussion.

Memoona Zahid is a poet and editor of Pakistani heritage, currently based in London. Her writing has appeared in various publications including *Tentacular, bath magg, Ink Sweat & Tears* and *Lumin Journal*. She is a Ledbury Poetry Critic and alumna of the University of East Anglia's Creative Writing Poetry MA. She is currently working on her first pamphlet.

ACKNOWLEDGMENTS

With thanks to:

The British Association for American Studies/United States Embassy Small Grants Programme; Economic and Social Research Council, Impact Acceleration Award; University of Glasgow Knowledge Exchange (KE) Small Grants 2020/21; City of London Grants; Museum of London Docklands; Ian & Clare Branagan; Dominic Christian; Ross and Caitlin Curtis; Matthew and Fiona Fosh; Tom and Caron Ilube; Kevin and Jennie Lee O'Donnell.

Core Partners

Runaway Slaves in Britain: bondage, freedom and race in the eighteenth century is a University of Glasgow project led by Professor Simon Newman which includes hundreds of runaway advertisements, as well as others offering enslaved people for sale, along with supporting materials. Professor Newman is the Sir Denis Brogan Professor of American History (Emeritus), and Honorary Professorial Research Fellow. Joining him on the Runaways London project is Dr. Peggy Brunache, a lecturer in the history of Atlantic slavery and Director of the Beniba Centre for Slavery Studies.

runaways.gla.ac.uk

Spread the Word is London's writer development agency, a charity and a National Portfolio client of Arts Council England. It aims to help London's writers make their mark on the page, the screen and in the world and build strategic partnerships to foster a literature ecology which reflects the cultural diversity of contemporary Britain. Spread the Word has a national and international reputation for initiating change-making research and developing programmes for writers that have equity and social justice at their heart.

spreadtheword.org.uk/runaways

Ink Sweat & Tears: an online poetry and prose web zine run by Kate Birch and edited by the poet Helen Ivory with a small print publishing arm whose pamphlets have been shortlisted for major poetry awards. Fahad Al-Amoudi, editor of this anthology, and Desree, who has also lent her expertise to the project, have been part of the Ink Sweat & Tears editing internship programme.

inksweatandtears.co.uk